Who says you're not good enou

You weren't born thinking 'I'm not good enough'. Someone or something made you feel that way, perhaps a long time ago.

Maybe your parents didn't praise you or show that they cared enough. Maybe your classmates were cruel about your shape, size or abilities. Maybe you expect so much of yourself that 'failure' is bound to happen.

Whichever way the idea got into your head, the fact is it's there now, and it's been rattling around for so long that you believe it.

When you believe you're no good, you start to behave as if it's true – hiding away, not trying new things, keeping quiet about what you want, apologising all the time, not bothering to look after yourself. All of which means you don't live or enjoy your life as much as you could.

But you can change. This book contains an easy plan for replacing bad ideas (like 'I'm no good') with much more sensible ones (like 'I'm alright really').

Turn the page and
see what happens

WELL DONE!

You chose to make a change

Keep doing that and your problems will soon be over.

How come? Well because it's so easy to believe ideas like "I'm useless"or "I'll never change". But these are just ideas that got in your head a while ago. If a different idea had got in there instead, like "I'm alright really", you wouldn't be reading this book.

So what we're going to do in the next few pages is show you how to develop positive ideas about yourself, and put them into your head, where they should have been all along.

Then, when you have a choice of things to believe, you can pick the right one, like you did a minute ago.

Sounds simple, doesn't it? So what are you going to do?

Keep reading - because change occurs step by step

YOU'RE GETTING GOOD AT THIS

So let's get some positive ideas going

If we told you the earth is flat, you wouldn't believe us, because you've been abroad and didn't drop off the edge. You have the evidence.

It's the same with ideas about yourself. It's hard to believe "I'm alright really" when you don't think you've got any evidence for it. So the first step in your plan is to spot some OK things about yourself and write them down.

Things you did well. Times you were helpful to others. Times you did something even when it was hard. Things you do that people thank you for. Things you know a lot about. Things you can do easily or quickly. Times when you make a good contribution to a group activity. People who like you… like that.

Turn over and list some OK things about yourself

Well done!

You turned to the OK Things list! It may take a while to come up with good stuff, because you've lost the habit of thinking you're OK. You are, though, so get writing!

Things I like about me

* Remember, we're looking for things you did well, times when you were helpful to others, people who like you and so on.

NOW LEARN YOUR LIST BY HEART

And say it to yourself whenever you feel small

You now have a list of reasons to believe you're OK, and every one is real and true, unlike those "I'm no good" ideas that sometimes come into your head.

Learn the list, and add more things to it as you think of them.

Keep repeating it so that it really sticks in your mind. Say it to yourself before going to sleep. Recite it quietly when you have a moment to yourself.

After a while, it will help to replace some of the negative ideas that have been hanging around for so long.

I'M OK
I'M OK

Even better, you can also use your list in emergencies, whenever you get into a situation that makes you feel small.

Just read the list over and over again and it will start to change the other stuff. It's just like you did on the last few pages, choosing a more sensible option instead of the "I'm useless" one.

Over the page is a chart that could help

Turn over for more help

DON'T THINK THIS

I can't do it

I'm not good looking

I'm boring

People don't like me

I'm not good at things

I mess everything up

THINK THIS

I can do it because I did
(something from your list)

I look just fine

I'm interesting, I know about
(something from your list)

Some people like me, including
(some people from your list)

I have strengths and weaknesses like everyone does

I'm good at
(something from your list)

So you know how to change how you think

What's next?

CHANGE WHAT YOU DO

How to build your confidence step by step

Everyone has an inside and an outside, and they're different.

You know those people who seem so confident? They're just like you inside, but they know a trick – walk confident, talk confident and you *become* confident.

So what you need to do is be yourself and make some small, steady changes to let the real you shine.

To begin with, take a good look at how you present to others. Think about:

1. What you wear.
2. How you stand.
3. What you say, and how you say it.

You'll also need to become very observant.

Now you get to make some changes

STEPS TO IMPROVING YOUR CONFIDENCE

How do other people do it?

Watch the way confident people stand. It's straight, isn't it? They often seem a bit taller than they really are.

Now pay attention to the way they hold themselves and move. There's no shuffling about, no slumping in chairs, no hiding in corners. And when they're speaking to you, they look you directly in the eye.

Now listen to the way they speak. They're pretty loud, aren't they? And they often speak quite slowly, not having to rush because they somehow know that everyone will keep on listening.

Your task is to slowly work towards this so people see the real you.

Remember, most confident people aren't like that all the way through, they just know how to act confident on the outside, which is what you'll be doing.

After a while you'll start to notice a real difference in how you present yourself.

Turn over for more helpful hints

DON'T DO THIS

Mumble

Talk too quickly

Slump in your chair

Hunch over

Look away or look down

Shut down conversations

DO
THIS

Try to speak a little louder and clearer

Slow down and pause while speaking

Sit up straight, shoulders back

Walk tall, lift your chin up

Make eye contact with others as much as possible, and smile

Ask questions to get conversations going

AM I UP TO THIS?

Yes, you are!

It sounds like a lot to do, doesn't it?
To change your thinking and then start
practising ways to become a more
confident you.

But you only have to do these things a little
bit at first. Make that list of things you like
about yourself,and just try reciting it once or
twice, when you feel small. Pick a confident
person and notice one of their mannerisms
to start with.

You won't become the life and soul of the
party overnight and you might not even
want to be that loud and bouncy anyway.

You're not here to become a big pop star or
a famous actor.

It's more about finding new ways to act
confident, but do it in your own style.

This way to a very
important thing

GOOD ENOUGH IS GOOD ENOUGH

Don't beat yourself up

In the real world, you don't have to get straight A's to be happy, successful and popular.

In fact the world's happiest people are those who are content with themselves as they are.

So whenever you're being hard on yourself for not doing something perfectly, not coming top of the class or finishing first in the race, say this to yourself -

There's no such thing as perfect. Just do what you can do.

YOU'RE
DOING
FINE

Here's how to stay that way

1. Choose sensible ideas not bad ones.
Fill in your list of things you like about you, learn it by heart and use it to change the negative ideas in your head.

Recite it to yourself before going to sleep. Use the list in situations that make you feel small and choose the "I'm OK" idea, not the "I'm useless" one.

2. Walk and talk with confidence.
Remember, most confident people aren't like that all the way through, they just know how to *act* confident on the outside.

So do the same. Walk confident, talk confident, look confident and you'll **be** confident.

3. Remember, there is no such thing as perfect. Just do what you can.
Nobody's perfect, so don't beat yourself up because you can't reach an impossible goal.

So, here's what to do. Pick one small thing, then use the *Planner* sheet on pages 26/27 to give yourself the best start.

Once you're done, use the *Review* sheet on pages 28/29 to check your progress.

Go for it!

Make a plan!
Planner Sheet

1. What am I going to do?

2. When am I going to do it?

3. What problems or difficulties could arise, and how can I overcome them?

Is my planned task -

	Yes	No
Q. Useful for understanding or changing how I am?	☐	☐
Q. Specific, so that I will know when I have done it?	☐	☐
Q. Realistic, practical and achievable?	☐	☐

How did it go?
Review Sheet

What did you plan to do? Write it here:

If yes:
1. What went well?

2. What didn't go so well?

3. What have you learned from what happened?

4. How are you going to apply what you have learned?

Yes **No**

Did you try to do it?

If no: what stopped you?

Internal things (forgot, not enough time, put it off, didn't think I could do it, couldn't see the point etc.).

External things (other people, work or home issues etc.).

How could you have planned to tackle these things?

WHERE TO GET EVEN MORE HELP

Sometimes "I'm not good enough" ideas are so deep seated that it's hard to work on them by yourself. That's when you need a bit more help than this little book can give.

For added help and support go to www.llttf.com. It's free and the number one site for low mood and anxiety recommended by NHS Trusts and teams in England.*

Having low confidence sometimes links in with other problems like worry, drinking too much, self-harm, not seeing friends, being scared to go out and other problems. This little book is a companion to all the ones on the right. When you've sorted your current problem, you might want to choose another little book and work on something else in your life.

*Bennion et al, 2017. BMJ Open http://bmjopen.bmj.com/content/7/1/e014844